Sister May I?

Written By: Danielle Chandler and Zoe Chandler
Illustrated By: Mirjana Bubevska

Sister May I
Copyright © 2025 by Danielle Chandler and Zoe Chandler

Written By: Danielle Chandler and Zoe Chandler
Illustrated By: Mirjana Bubevska

Publisher: Imagine Write Now, LLC
www.sharifabrown.com

All rights reserved. No part of this publication may be reproduced or transmitted in any form without written permission of the both author and publisher, except for the use of brief quotations in a book review.

ISBN: 979-8-9880058-6-5 Paperback
ISBN: 979-8-9880058-7-2 Hardback

This book is dedicated to all of the sisters who were born with a "built in best friend". As you grow up and time will pass, remember that your sisterly love will always last.

⭐ Danielle Chandler and Zoe Chandler

Meet the Authors!

Danielle and Zoe may be young, but they already have a powerful gift—storytelling! At just 8 and 12 years old, these two sisters have written Sister May I, a book that reflects their love for each other and the incredible adventures they create using their imaginations. Growing up as inseparable siblings, they have spent countless hours making up stories, dressing up as different characters, and creating their own little worlds. Now, they're excited to share their story with readers everywhere, hoping to inspire other children to embrace their creativity and treasure the bond of family.

SISTERS

I love my big sister, she's my very best friend.
We do everything together, and the fun never ends.
She's always protecting me and teaching me what's right.
She's the best big sister, I never let her out of my sight.

I always wanted a sister, a built-in best friend.
My wish finally came true, someone to love, dress up, and play pretend.
I was so excited the day my little sister came home.
From that moment on, I promised her that she would never be alone.

Sister! Sister! May I play? May I play with you and your friends today?
Well of course sister you may play, you can play with us every day!
Sister! Sister! May I go? May I go with you, please don't say no!
Well of course sister you may go, it will be such a fun show!

Sister! Sister! That was so much fun, let's do it again tomorrow since the day is done.

Sister! Sister! The gang's all here! We are ready for laughs and cheer!
I wonder where we will go today, wherever it is, let's not delay!

Sis, I think that maybe you should stay.
Why don't you play with your friends today?
I don't want to be mean and make you feel sad,
but this time you stay home, please don't be mad.

Sister! Sister! It's always been you and me. Please can I go with you? Pretty, pretty, pretty please!
I'll be quiet, you won't even know I'm there, as long as I'm with you, I'll stay out of your hair!

You are my little sister and you have brought me the most joy I have ever known, but sometimes I really just want to be alone.

We can play whatever you want when I get home later.
We can have some ice cream too, you can pick the flavor!

No fair! I always come with you wherever you go, what's different now, you have never told me no!

Sister! Sister! Today at school, I met someone new! Her name is Michelle, I'll introduce her to you.
Sister, I can't wait to meet her, I know she's super cool, it's so great to meet new friends at school.

What's all the excitement, did something special happen today? You sure do have a lot to say!
Sister! May I tell Mom and Dad the good news?!
Let me sis, it has me jumping out of my shoes!

Today we were class partners and even sat together at lunch,
we both love the same things,
especially cookies and fruit punch!
I talked a lot about you and all the fun things we do, she told me that she has a big sister too!

I can hardly wait for our play date we are planning together, maybe skating or the park, we can go wherever!

Well that is pretty special, do you see what a simple "hello" can do! Yes honey, meeting new friends doesn't have to be scary and soon enough, you'll be stuck together like glue!

No one told me that meeting new friends is so much fun! So much fun, you can't have just one!
But I'll always want to spend time with my big sis, when we are apart, you are surely missed!

You may have found new friends to run, jump and play, always know I'll be right here, never too far away.

Sister, may we go and play, just you and I?
Well of course sister, let's go play, I hope the time doesn't fly!

As sisters, there will be issues that come and go, but if we face them together, our love will grow.
You are my very best friend and I know that sometimes you need your time and space, but we'll always be sisters, a bond that no one can break.

Who knows, maybe you will get the chance to be a big sister one day, having someone that looks up to you in every single way!

www.ingramcontent.com/pod-product-compliance
Lightning Source LLC
Chambersburg PA
CBHW041135130526
44582CB00031B/136